Low-_lying Balloons

Mike Gower

STEPHEN MORRIS

To my grandchildren Zeph and Flora

STEPHEN MORRIS

First published in 2024 by Stephen Morris
www.stephen-morris.co.uk
smc@freeuk.com

ISBN 978-1-7396050-9-4

British Library Cataloguing-in-Publication Data
A catalogue record for this book is available from the British Library

Design and typesetting © Stephen Morris 2024
set in Hoefler Text 10/13.5

Contents

Acknowledgements

My gratitude to every poet who has
interested, excited, and moved me; to
friends, and especially to my partner Ann,
who have criticised and encouraged my
work; to fellow Lansdown poets; to Bob
Walton, Bristol's mover and shaker of many
fine poetry events, and to Stephen Morris,
my publisher, for his expertise and
imagination.

Adam and Eve It

'Now, let me tell you a story,' said Adam.

'No, it wasn't like that at all,' said Eve.

'Do you really want to know the truth?' said the Snake.

'As victim (I got eaten) ask me,' said the Apple.

The Tree said, 'Believe what you find.

That will be your story.'

Where to Start?

Start with this stream –
satyr, it goat-hoofs over rocks,
stone-steps, flickers light.

On the rough path, a dor beetle,
shining parade-boot black,
advances on six-legged tracks.

On the bank,
a baby's soft fist of a fern tip
is curled to unfurl.

Guest of the warm sun,
I sit, back propped by the base of a silver birch,
and observe the wild wood's absence
of set-squares, rulers

but find in movement and growth
a science which cancels no beauty.

Thomas, my doubting friend,
thrust your hand into this moss:
believe.

Jellyfish in Loch Kinaird

You hang in water
canopy of perfect parachute,
transparent mushroom flexing
like gentle breathing.
Suddenly you are a shoal
besieging my small craft;
my oars dip and swirl your forms.
Are you aquatic angels,
or used condoms?
You are tasselled upside-down lampshades;
and – submarine – diaphanous umbrellas.

But this makar's metaphors fail;
I lack hooks to catch you,
keep nets to hold.
I leave you your sea loch and –
unjelly, unfish –
pull for the foot-firm shore.

Woodpecker

Woodpecker
no tree breaker
but hole hammerer
through bark to bole
vibrating like a stammer, steam hammer.
Neck flex of muscle, boxer's skull
strong enough to take the shock,
the knockknockknockknock knockknockknockknock
of pneumatic drill.
No bird freak
this avian with a steel beak.

He drops to my lawn
to mine for ants, and cocks an eye
to the sky – but who would dive-bomb
this tough guy? He's no rom-com.

Now he's up and away over the fence,
flash of green, but for me no past tense
but rhythm-in-my-head,
Black and DDDDecker
woodpecker.

Toothstone

I bit a plumstone,
it broke my tooth –
little enamelled stone
that I spat out.

I passed a wall –
a stone, fallen, had left
a hole like a lost tooth –
the stone lay grounded.

The wall still stands,
my mouth makes the best of it.
Repairs are possible –
dentist, stonemason.

Carved

In Bristol Cathedral, at the top of an arch, the carved head of a woman. She is not gazing submissively heavenward. She does not look particularly holy. To me she suggests another story.

I am stone
lived once
was beaten
wed
beaten again
knew childbirth
died of cancer
the usual things.

Unusual
the itinerant
stonemason
our love.

He raised me
here on this arch
looking down on the nave
and the people
who know no better
and the priests
who are no better.

I don't see them.
I see only
wood
stream
sky
our tryst.

Man

The express train tore by.
It created noise, a churning wind,
a momentary blotting out of landscape.
Then it dwindled and disappeared
down its twin steel rulers.
What did it leave?

Everything much as it was,
except perhaps for the man trespassing,
standing by the rail.
Was it closeness and shock that he searched for,
dramatic sensation so strong
that it would obliterate all else?
Was it to assert life?
Or had he meant to step forward,
bow knee and head,
decapitate his troubles?

Yet he stood there still.
I called to him, 'Adam!'
He turned to me crying,
'Don't talk to *me* about fuckin' Eve!'

In the Classroom

In the classroom
the child sits silent,
her teacher furious
that she does not listen,
will not learn.
The teacher takes it personally.

In the classroom
the girl, secretly abused, pregnant,
dumb with shame and fear,
suddenly screams at the teacher,
taking it personally.

Inheritance

'Here, have this,' we say to the child.
'You'll need that too, doesn't it glitter?
We want you to have a sweet life
so suck on this. Don't worry,
we've lots of experience to keep
the money rolling in – our way.
We'll leave you a heritage. Take no notice
of those silly people who bang on about
sewage swamping our rivers, soil impoverishment,
glaciers melting, wildfires, wars, floods, famines –
it'll all sort out; we know what we're doing.
Stick to your smartphones, eyes down
and you won't notice a thing.
We're really leaving you a heritage.
Well then, say thank you.'

The Butterfly Book

I opened the butterfly book
and all the butterflies flew out:
peacocks, red admirals, painted ladies,
fritillaries, small powder blues
beat their soft flights about my head,
made silent eddies in the air,
then settled on my shoulders,
arms, chest, thighs and
– most softly – on my face.
They quivered with warmth.

A voice summoned me to tea.
I sighed, shut them back
in the book, then stretched up
to fit it in its place on the shelf.

At tea, I dutifully chewed my apple.

RUNNING!
– boy, 1945, London E17

Seven years old
Leaning on his hands in the basin's warm water
gazing up the road opposite
coloured blue, red, yellow
depending which way he leans
to look through which coloured pane,
delightful power ...
when he should be hurrying -
late for school again!

RUNNING

up Howard Road, North London grey
('There is a war on, you know!')
37,39, *41!*
Bang on the knocker,
little ginger Granny – ready – opening the door

RUNNING

through the house, out of the kitchen,
down the back garden path,
bump, bump, bump down three steps,
grab-pull the wooden gate
slam it behind him

RUNNING

up Aubrey Road
swing left, first small terraced house
Bang-bang on the door. Johnny Mendam
(family of nine, Dad a lorry-driver) ready,

RUNNING

past the bomb site,
past Ruby Road where lives Reenie Bolton
his seven-year-old-eternal-love
along the long curve of Greenway Road, then

BANG!!

a V2 rocket hits four roads away
flat on their faces on the dust grey paving
then up and

RUNNING

it's all a game
school gates, teachers with whistles
children lined up, final dash to sidestep-shove
into their class queue
in the right alphabetical order, and

NOT RUNNING

panting, grinning, ready for
whatever comes *next.*

Beat

Somewhere hearts *will* beat
to the old iambic rhythm
th-UMP th-UMP th-UMP
in the cold of cave
in the scorch of desert
in the echoing catacomb even
somewhere a heart still beats

There and there and there and *then*
From motionless slime to the power of pulsing
New-formed beat of hearts
as rhythm of sunrise, sunfall
contracting, expanding, heart's pumping.

Here and here and there and now
rhythm of feet, treading of sand dune
paving, field, tarmac, forest
rhythm of bodies in dance
rhythm of hearts pounding, pounding
the animal, the human, the animal human
Now know the beat in the heart of the World.

Boxer

Like rugby (head impacts) or soccer (heading the ball),
boxing (getting thumped) is rightly considered a hazard to
the brain, and is now generally discouraged. Yet, as a boy
and young man, amateur boxing gave me discipline,
confidence and sporting pleasure trying to outwit and
outmanoeuvre my opponent – as he was trying to do to me
– on equal grounds. In that sense it was remarkably like
squash or tennis – or even chess.

Left jab, right cross,
left hook, right hook,
uppercut – five good punches,
keeping on your toes,
moving, watching, gloves held high,
ready to slip or block, duck or weave,
instant with the counterpunch,
wary, but combative, looking for the opening,
not leaving him an opening,
pace the fight, build the points,
know when to hang on;
if down, watch the count,
up at eight, use the ring, keep out of trouble
till your head clears, then,
as he gets cocky, over-confident
hit him hard, again, again, again –
down on the canvas for ten.
job well done. Referee raises your hand;
step to your opponent's corner in courtesy,
acknowledge your supporters,
duck under the ropes, jump down from the ring,
thank your trainer, get a shower, change.

Now you can relax, drink, have a meal,
have fun with friends, with your girlfriend.

Tomorrow get on with ordinary life,
but the day after, back into training:
running, punchbag, listening to your coach,
sparring, thinking, sweating: hard work,
getting ready for your next fight.

Jazz 1

Jazz

    born black, ripped out of old Africa,
    chained cargo, marketed as cattle,
    slaves to sorrow, to outrage, to America,
    but begetting soul and body of the Blues,
    and the Blues begat

Jazz

Jazz 2

Jazz

    a quiet conversation between three.

Jazz

    a band of five pilgrims sharing a journey.

Jazz

    a blow up, a rip up, a wild storm of seven.

Jazz

    big band bonding, burgeoning rhythms,
    tones, tunes, textures, colours, a break out
    as a rugby team, each player his role
    to lock, heave, drive, fling out, race for the line,
    celebrating music of muscle, brain, heart.

Jazz!

Vibrato

When that I was but a little tiny boy,
With a heigh-ho the wind and the rain
I sang too in a church choir, my voice
fine as gossamer, clear as a moorland spring,
an icicle in cold sunlight....
Then my balls dropped,
my voice croaked and squeaked
unpredictable as adolescence.

Now, full of years and bad decisions,
biffs and bangs, wear and tear,
too many bars, too many beers,
hear me, a baritone seen better days,
a voice for Lear if not Methuselah,
A voice vibrating, rusty, smokey black diesel.

(My mother said that Louis Armstrong's voice was
'dirty' – yes Ma, I'm getting there!)

Gossamer snaps,
spring water downstream melds with sewage,
icicles drip like cold noses in the wind.
Yet we hear good vibrations: Charles Aznavour,
Bessie Smith, Sonny boy Williamson
and the Blessed Edith Piaf. Their rich tremors
are strength, depth of soul, a Fifth Dimension.

May our voices too make tremble the listening air.

Hull Down

He wrote in praise
Of Bessie Smith
And Billie Holiday
From his jazz heart.

That heart, mind
And those flat feet
Were not approved by all
But writing poems

As he did and showing
Love and admiration
For those black women
And their jazz

He can't have been
Such a bad-arse man
That poet man
That Philip Larkin.

Sir Gawain and the Green Knight: Addendum

Sir Gawain and the Green Knight is a wonderful late-14th-century story in a northern dialect. It's a subtle marriage of courtly manners and honour, an epic winter trek and an outrageous challenge to the Court of King Arthur by the mysterious and awesome Green Knight: 'Here's a party game for you. Who has the courage to chop off my head now, and, in a year's time, set out to find me and be, in turn, decapitated?'

1   Who is the hero, Sir G or the GK?
       The lady in the Castle, or Morgan la Faye?
       Or maybe the wodwo? Tell it another way!

2   The best parties need a challenge,
       something unexpected, dramatic,
        some magical realism, maybe the impossible.
       Enter the Green Knight!

3   (Later, I want Sir Gawain to be seduced:
       his host's Lady is witty, charming, beautiful,
       and she sits on his bed and requests a kiss.
       She says he's the Knight to best all knights.
       But what penalty awaits!)

4   If I were Sir Gawain
       I would answer to the Green Knight's challenge,
       'Sod off! Don't spoil the King's party.'
       But he clearly has ... Or has he?
       A party to remember?
       Oh, yes, I was there!

The Pardoner

From The Prologue to *The Canterbury Tales*

Created a good 630 years ago, Chaucer's characters remain vital and, in this instance, outrageous. It was a delight to try a fresh translation attempting – I repeat – attempting, to catch the subtlety of his satire.

With us
There was a PARDONER from Rouncivale
– he was, I guess, the Summoner's best pal –
come swiftly from the Papal Court of Rome.
In treble voice he sang, "My love, come home
to me".The Summoner backed him with a roar
Of deepest bass, no tuba sounded more.
This Pardoner had hair peroxide blond
And it hung smooth and long, and he was fond
Of tossing it about his shoulders narrow –
It could have made a nest for wren or sparrow.
For fun and fashion's sake he wore no hood,
He thought his style was cool and super-good.
But with his hair so fashionable and fair
He had a staring eye much like a hare.
His manbag lay before him on his knee
Brimful of pardons straight from Papal See
Oven-fresh and hot as new baked cakes.
His voice was thin as a goat's bleat makes.
He had no beard, his chin was smooth and bare –
I guess he was gelding or a mare.
But of his skill from Berwick down to Ware
There was no one to match this Pardoner,
For in his bag he had a pillowcase

Which, he swore, had veiled Our Lady's face.
He said he had a fragment of the sail
Of Peter's boat when Christ (you know the tale)
Walked on the Sea of Galilee in stormy rout
And Saviour Jesus had to fish him out.
He had a cross of latten stuck with stones;
Stashed in a bottle he had old pigs' bones.
But with these relics when he caught
Poor farming peasants quite untaught
In just one day he'd screw more gelt
Than in eight weeks the parson ever smelt.
And so, with false flattery and jokey japes,
He made a fool of parson, and of people, apes.
But, when all is said and truly done,
In Church he could have been a bishop's son.
He was first-rate at reading Bible stories,
Yet best of all he sung the offertories.
He knew full well that when he'd lisped that song
His turn would come to preach with silver tongue
And coins would clink like bells are rung –
That's why so keenly and so merrily he sung.

Emily Dickinson Met...

Emily Dickinson
met the Simpsons.
She saw homo sapiens:
homo in Homer,
sapiens in Marge,
and herself in Lisa.

Emily Dickinson
travelled in a spacecraft.
She nodded to the Moon,
told Mars to control himself,
exchanged verses with Venus,
and thought Outer Space worth a visit.

Emily Dickinson
encountered Attila the Hun.
He was surprised that she stood her ground.
She said, 'I am the ground.
I like your horse. Who are you?'

Emily Dickinson
bumped into Samuel Beckett.
She said, 'What took you so long?'

Slug

My home-grown lettuces are blond and beautiful,
a neat row of perfections plumped.
Pull one, and between crisp leaves find small grey
slugs, lettuce predators, their black excrement
like damp soot flakes, your anticipated salad
slimed and shat upon. What to do?

Cut away the lower half, pull off the outer leaves,
find a travesty of what first pleased your eyes.
Stamp the slugs flat on your patio. Wash and wash
the remaining leaves. You rage at nature's greed?
Accept that we too are lettuce eaters,
a species of upright and self-righteous slug.

Gulps x 10

In Eden, Adam grabbed the apple from Eve
and wolfed it whole.
He was the *first* fast-food man.

Now you can drive into
the Billy Bunter Belly Buster Burger Bar,
buy, gobble and bugger off.

And food is *produced* fast: pump-feed with antibiotics
and watch, in their concentration camp,
a million chickens' legs buckle as they swell.

No need to waste time cooking –
buy a plastic packet packed with e-numbers,
microwave, and then down it goes – gulp, gone!

Loving him, she spent hours cooking his meal.
He wolfed it down and burped.
Later, in bed, he farted.

French people are silly: they waste time
cooking. They indulge in long lunch breaks,
socialising over food – it's only fuel!

2 millennia ago, it seems, bread
and wine sufficed for the 12 + 1. But where
Was Mary Magdalene? Oh, still baking.

Mind, go to your supper with a clear conscience
or, like Macbeth, you may meet a blast from the past.
It will quite spoil your appetite.

What an irony that we also use the word 'fast'
for *not* eating. Now here's a niche opportunity –
Fast-Food Fasting!

Let us then relish and savour our food,
but let us strive to see that *all* people are fed well.
Good. Now pass me that bar of chocolate!

Political Pamphlet

I guided, pushed, poked,
shoved through letterbox flaps
our Political Pamphlet.
It said how our Party was Right
and how the others were Wrong.
From the cover page smiled
our white-toothed candidate.
I delivered hundreds.

One came back, shoved crumpled
through my letter-flap,
a chosen sentence underlined,
and, scrawled alongside, the word
Bollocks.
My heart lifted –
someone had read it,
someone had read it critically.

Now that
is democracy.

It's Normal
day return ticket

Temple Meads Station
(iron, glass, steel)
Is a curved cathedral
Dedicated to Saint Steam
Who, like miracles, is dead.

But not so:
Clear and disembodied
A vaulted voice announces that
At Stapleton Road Station
My train will turn into a bus.

At Avoncliffe Halt
You stop the train
By waving to it.
I try it.
It stops.

My train this morning
Was held up between Redland and Montpelier
by low-flying balloons.

So miracles are not dead.

Many trains run on time.

Recycling

Just married,
we had no furniture –
except the bed.
From the builders' merchants over the back wall
I bought a plank – for £1.

Next morning it grinned at me
With a twist and a new split up its grain.
Still, I sawed, drilled, screwed, and made a bench for two.
Ambitious, we bought a table from a third-hand shop;
So, we could sit, spread our books and papers,
then elbow them aside to eat.
The bench was hard; cushionless,
we rocked from buttock to buttock,
but it served while your belly grew with baby –
while our babies grew through stroppy adolescence,
and then took academic flight.

After, they took unto them men, and made homes
– short of furniture. One daughter took the bench.
Doubtless, she and her man shifted weight
from left buttocks to right to left – but it served.

Then they bought good chairs.
So, at the strong hands of our daughter's man,
the bench was unbenched and reinvented,
raised and replanted on the wall.
Proudly it bears books again,
shrugs its warped shelf-shoulder,
and still grins its grainy shake.

What It Isn't Like

No, not even similar to.
Yet I still think of trees lashed by wind,
litter launched skywards, battling cyclists,
and black birds blown from horizon to horizon.
Is it the wind or all that it does?

Nor is it similar to
the city's usual traffic jam: miles of boredom, frustration,
bonnet to exhaust pipe, all that CO_2 from idling engines,
idling minds. Nor pedestrians shuffling or striding, figures
talking to their phones, figures of speech.

So what is it similar to?
Now here's the problem: the thing is the thing,
though it depends from what angle, in what light.
When it moves its context alters, it alters.
Well, I'll leave it there. Let me know if you find it.
Tell me what it's like.

This is not
or, Weasel Words

This is not a Water Feature.
It is deep, muddy, duck-weedy,
frogged, tadpoled, newted, with wild iris –
It is a POND.

This is not a Utility Room.
Here I wash greasy dishes, smelly clothes, muddy parsnips,
shelves spill with tools and tidbits.
It is a SCULLERY.

That is not a Sports Utility Vehicle.
It is broad, boastful, diesel guzzling, road hogging,
street bullying (is that a sport?)
It is a JUGGERNAUT.

This is not a Military Exercise.
It is lies, murder, rape, mayhem,
genocide, madness.
It is WAR.

This is not a Literary Exercise.
It is a POEM.

Flat Earth

You gotta believe it.
I mean, if the World was round
most of us would fall off it.
That's why I voted Brexit.

And another thing, if it's round
all the seas, and your beer, would spill.
I mean, there's gravity for you.
Nigel Farage understands that.

Oh yeah, I've crossed the Channel
to France for ciggies and booze
but they talk foreign. I say
speak English – that's natural, innit!

When it comes down to it
the Earth's gotta be flat – common sense.
True Brits don't bend,
and that's why I love Brexit!

Latest, Biggest

I saw an SUV
latest number plate, new, bigger;
red and black, it snarled,
loomed large, macho.

Big Bull King, status One,
Behemoth
it commandeered the tired
and narrow tarmac.

Then I saw the stretches,
the MPVs and polished pickups
cosseting a family and their packed and piled essential
holiday possessions.

Presence, power,
wealth, assertion.
I wondered who the drivers were
and how proud they must be feeling

in their accumulating traffic jam
stretching
        to the Planet's
                end.

Set in Concrete
Eperlecques, Nord-pas-de-Calais

Walk with me up this path through the Autumn wood.
Birds go about their aerial business,
And that dragonfly, metallic blue,
Darts left, right, patrolling space that's his.
He will not harm us. Let's turn this corner, and

Blockhaus!
A million tons of concrete, death-grey, sheer fortress.
Pre-stressed rusted rods sprout like mad hair
From fractured blocks. Out of warm sunlight,
The great steel doors gone, we enter inner darkness.
Stench of stagnant water. We look up, up
At vast ruined pillars. Here is the cathedral of the damned.

Raised to spawn the V2 rocket, the super weapon
Drinking liquid oxygen, exhaling fire,
Blasting to the stratosphere, the six minute curve
Of unstoppable descent, to explode on London's people.

There was a fighting back of bombers, black silhouettes
As ack-ack spat fireworks. And Eperlecques was hit.
Though no bombs could penetrate the massive concrete
Of the inner walls, they sparked an earthquake
That so shook the rockets and their lethal liquid fuels
That Nazi scientists did the one sane thing – they ran.
But come, look closer at these inner walls:
They bear the grain and knots and natural imperfections
Of every plank that shuttered the once wet concrete.

Here is a fossil, a fingerprint, a history of once-living wood
Wielded by the forced bodies that built this blockhaus.
Three thousand, of many tongues, enslaved.
Bravely, some sabotaged machinery and were hanged.
The rest were starved, beaten.

Now on the sour concrete, grained by the planks,
Touch stigmata of their broken hands.

The Leader

Napoleon's Grande Armée
set out for Russia in smart uniforms,
well armed and trained, used to victory.
They found Moscow burning
and dark Winter pouring over the horizon.
The Retreat cut down their pride.
Ambushed, starving, frost-bitten,
boots worn through, they limped,
and fell. A jackal populace tore them apart.
Napoleon, on his fine horse,
rode on.

Plums And Passchendaele

In the night, the great bough of my plum tree crashed
felled by wind and the weight of its fruit –
not yet ripe, but hundredfold.

At Passchendaele – mud, misery and crashing artillery –
by insane order men charged machine guns.
Unripe, they fell thousandfold.

I sealed my tree's split wound. The grounded bough lay
attached by a sliver. Weeks later, leaves still fresh,
I pick and eat its ripe fruit.

Nature heals.
War does not.

On Parade

Passchendaele's cemeteries: immaculate geometry,
gravestones 'right-dressed' in perfect order,
all on parade, every stone present and correct
and silent for God's inspection.

Unlike war's chaos: bawled orders drowned by barrage
of artillery, stench of shit and rotting corpses,
mud blood-reddened, men's curses, screams.
Out of mis-order, hell's anarchy.

Passchendaele's cemeteries: respect or mockery?

Your Buried Ashes

You lie under the young pear tree,
you rise through roots, trunk, branches.
Beside you, our dog's fine skeleton
rests deep, still company.

All things grow: the even rows
of the ordered, the hand-planted,
but also wild-sown weeds,
their quick chaos, their anarchy.

At my left shoulder
trains pendulate;
at my right shoulder
tidal sweep of the Avon.

Working this soil
I breathe your breath
who is earth
and sweet fruit of the pear.

Trees x 7: a collage

Stand beneath this oak,
look up, up.
Admire.
Climb it if you can.

> 'Out of strength came forth sweetness.'
> The beech, felled,
> dead across the forest floor,
> flourishes with fungi.
> In its rotting hollows insects build cities
> cosmopolitan, teeming.

Chipboard: sawdust and glue –
we render down arboreal dignity.

> In the wet yard
> stacked timber
> gleams under rain.

Wooden sheds, basic, battered
tilting on the allotments' slope
keeping tools dry.

A wonder on Borth Beach:
current and tide conspire
to sweep sand clear revealing
a black stump forest.
My Jack Russell sees big sticks,
sinks his teeth into wood
eight thousand years old.
'Billy, NO!'

Son of carpenter becomes carpenter,
Inherits plane, saw, chisel.
Strong fingers, muscled forearms create
chair, table, bed, roof beams.
He abandons workshop for the rude road
and greater works.
But what rough hewer, nailer
cobbles his cross?

From Writer to Reader

She's writing
        a novel...

an acorn
        sprouting
to sapling
        growing
to mighty oak
        branches
multiple
        leaf full
networking
        the sky...

I climb it.

Nor' Easter on Rodway Common

If it had a passport this wind's
Distinguishing marks would be *thin and cold*.
Its photo would be sharp, unsmiling and invisible.
There is uncertainty about its place of birth:
Stockholm, Helsinki might do, but it has a glacial smell,
a touch of Arctic Russia, begot
on a desperate night in Murmansk:
father unemployed and drunk, mother
drunk and unemployed – at minus forty.
It learned no small talk over Finland's frozen lakes,
no social graces as it coursed the rusting carcass
of industry in Kaliningrad. Over Denmark it brushed
the luxury of brightly coloured warm clothes
and was not impressed. It kicked up
some North Sea waves but left fish to swim
as best they could round oily pipes
and giant skeletons of rigs. It entered England
through a grimy port, its harbour
more full of bobbing litter than of fishing boats;
and – to cut a cold journey short – this wind
met me on Rodway Common. It spat
small snowflakes and rattled some
last dry leaves on the frozen path.
I looked it straight in the face, no flattery.

It whipped tears from my eyes,
but I was glad. This wind-without-passport,
this freezing comer-and-leaver,
this new-ageless traveller without baggage
brought re-knowledge of an ancient rhythm of the world
which grunts, turns in its sleep and settles
to a deeper breathing. Here,
in this cold wind's cut and penetration
of the bare forked tree, of the poor bare forked animal
is a truth beyond the wind of words.

No Hiding

Lear on the heath
Born at eighty
Burning and blown through
Like fire
Like flames of ice
The bellows and blasts
Whip the wild words
Rip the wild heart
The streaming hair
The brain turning, turning
Beating its bone walls
No palace, no hovel
Is hiding-place
Is resting place
There is no hiding place

But into this cry-chaos
This cut-deep, this cauter
Comes love, gently...

Comes love cruelly as death
And limp in your arms
Oh Cordelia ...

Shakespeare Shows Us

Shakespeare shows us evil
on the apron stage.
Insolent Iago steps forward, confides in us.
We listen, wrapt.
Thereafter, each 'honest' word
slipped like mercury into Othello's ear
we know for what it is.
We do not stop it.
We do not cry, 'Behind you!'
Fascinated we watch Cassio gullible,
Othello credulous, Desdemona undone,
Iago focussed.
We do not stop it.
It is a play we pay to see
and when Iago's deeds are done
and all struck down,
Virtue rises, the just Law
sentences, and he, the torturer,
meets his torture.
We are satisfied, replete.
Applauding, we rise and step
four centuries into our world
of war and ethnic cleansing,
starvation, slavery.
And shall we stop it?

The Merchant of Venice

Does *anyone* come out of this well?
The flower of the youth of Venice?
Oh, such gentillesse as they spit
upon his Jewish gabardine! And,
for all her finesse and first-rate legal brain,
Portia is no critic of the anti-semitic.
And sweet Jessica? A petty thief
who'll switch religion as turn a leaf.

Shylock himself? His Justice is revenge,
and he'd gladly carve a christian. His knife
is keen for goyim blood. He is parody of usurer,
yet at the end, though I'd not trust him
for a friend, and he's no tragic hero,
I have a feeling for this underdog
whom they call *dog*, whose ruin and humiliation
is cause for celebration in a vicious Venice.

Is that him knocking at my door?
Well, welcome. Come on in.

13 Ways of Looking at Stones
after Wallace Stevens

He didn't drop like a stone
but fell like flying that had failed
and crying, crying a word
too late to hear –
he broke on the stones beneath.

She gave love,
adulterous, but love.
Their eyes gleamed
with the gang rape of stoning.
It took one man who knew love
to shame them.

Cadaver rots and stinks,
wood perishes,
nails and brass corrode,
but the stone weathers
in the commune of the churchyard –
feathers of June grass caress it.

In my head is a stone.
In my heart is a stone.
It is now the end of our touching.

She is homeless and hungry
at the end of her tether.
She cries for bread
to the lords of our land
who give her a stone.

You threw the first cheek
but I turned the other stone.

To speak my joy of you ninefold
I skim the flattest pebble on the beach
over nine waves of our passion – it skips nine times.

The hammer and the chisel
and the hand and the stone
chip, chip, chip,
into a cathedral.

I would wish all billionaires in their Bentleys
to take off their shoes
and walk the stoney path home.
Would their children welcome them?

Lift the stone
and admire the society that lives under it.
Replace it gently.

There is nothing dry
about this stone wall:
lichens live on it,
small things dart and hide
in this their city.

The sibilant sea is in love
with its clattering opposite,
flows naked up the beach,
draws pebbles chittering to its depths:
oh, such desire –
again
and again
like breathing.

I split the stone in two and see,
curled like a baby waiting to be born,
the ammonite.
Across a hundred million years
it touches my finger.

Living on Levels

Living on levels,
digging from stratum to stratum,
or climbing deck to deck,
mixing metaphors like sand and cement
(or chalk and cheese), always
the grass will be greener.

But no, let's rest here,
enough of ear-popping ascents, descents,
let's for now settle
with this one slice of living.

And this is the quiet one,
almost silent.
Like eyes adopting to dark
the sounds come like shy animals:
faint flutter and pop of the fire,
the clock's neat heartbeat,
a baby crying its anger or hunger
but walls away.

I've always wanted a lower stratum,
to enter the ship's belly,
or delve into the earth,
and, adjusting, hear the rustle of roots,
the sigh of decaying loam...
then the thrash of the worm,
and thunder of pursuing mole.

The Poor Poet finds a Metaphor to Metamorphose the Beast into Beauty

Scavengers come bottom of the castes –
untouchables,
the dung beetles of rotting carcasses.
They are ugly with it:
the hyena, hump-shouldered and man-trap jawed
skulks round the lion's kill;
vultures, scrag-necked
hop obscenely, scrapping to gouge an eye,
no Queensbury Rules observed.
Even my dog,
fed best tinned doggyfood
in his shiny-clean doggybowl,
will wrench at his lead
to guzzle some black, unnameable
splodge on the pavement.

Yet the rhythm of the hyena pack
rolls the treadmill veldt,
road runners who need no road.
Vultures drift like smoke
from mountain roosts, and circle
effortless as eagles.
My boot and nose shy from
the stinking carcass,
but my eye catches
the dung beetle's back
shining clean as the sun.

I thought it might be fun to write acrostic poems with my grandchildren. It was.

Zebra

Zipped stripes, white-and-black-jack,
Equine from spine to hoof, horse-toothed,
Built for savannah, Africana,
Ripe to run in herd race over wide-open space -
Avoid gun, shun lion, trust no-one under hot sun.

VOLE

Very small fur ball, bright eyes, whirring legs to scurry and twinkle
Over, round, under
Litter of leaf and log (watch out for weasel, owl, dog)
Endlessly searching for finnicles, insecticles – luscious vole victuals.

KESTREL

King of keepy-uppy in the air
Easy held station wings aquiver
Solo hunter with super sight searching for supper
Targets twitch of a grass blade
Radar ready to recognise rodent
Eyes lock-on to exact pinpoint, then
Lances down – lightning strike – claws claim catch!

KIWI

Krazy kiwi, like a fruit on two legs,
In antipodean forests, nocturnal hunter -
Watch out all nations, he's king of the rugby,
Incredible islander, squeaker and squawker of NZ nights.

DUCK

Duck, head-diver, tail to the stars,
Under-water dabbler of waving green weeds,
Catch-what-you-can in the wash of the waters,
Keep company – duck 'n' drake – conjugal *quacks*.

SPIDER

Spun silk web, dewfall-drenched, trembles as I touch.
Predator arachnid parks off stage pretending passivity.
Innocent ignorant fly struggles enmeshed –
Death is life, fly is spider's dinner.
Everyone must eat, excepting no-one, each to his edibles.
Repeat: we all eat – veg, fruit or meat. Treat!!

Imagine

Imagine a mute swan
hovering overhead in full song,

or a raven turning up its beak in disdain
at something only recently slain,

or a Canada goose
the size of a moose,

or a robin
sobbin' its heart out,

or a woodpecker, its one and only goal
to fill a tree hole,

or a big white gannet
waddling all the way from the Isle of Thanet
and when you offer it a dish
it says, 'No thank you, I don't eat fish.'

All this would be quite unnatural
and not at all factual
– but a lot of fun!

Legs

Wings and fins are fine things, but on dry land,
earth, rock, mud and sand, steppe or forest,
plank or paving stone there is much to be said
for legs. The norm is six – ask any ant.
Spiders insist on eight. Centipedes prefer –
well, the clue is in the name. Mammals favour four –
not the whaley ones who thrash a monstrous tail,
but four as in 'four corners of the Earth' (though round),
or 'four square' (though animals abhor the cube).
But in mammalian maths, four is twice as good as two.
Some use legs s l o w l y as giant sloths;
many are shifty – see leopard pursuing antelope.
Some lumber like elepotami, or crawl like crocodiles,
Others whizz as little lizards or 100 milesperhour mice.

But we – poor homo saps – make do with two.
However though and then, this does give us advantages,
frees our front legs to work with pen and keyboard,
hammer and tongs, spatula and spade, pick-your-pocket,
gesticulate our love, or punch a nose.

This leaves us balancing as on a two-pronged fork;
so take my hand, my Love, and let our four legs walk.

Crow

Crow
not really so
as Ted Hughes' visceral black joker nightmare.
Let's be fair:
crow is a jobbing flap flap flap
down flop, clown hop,
'Caw!' his one note rap,
less artful dodger
than general bodger,
a shoveller up of splurged road kill -
disgusting, but he'll eat his fill,
not a high flier,
more a worn tyre.

He's a sort of success,
no more no less,
but just so
is crow.

13 Ways of Looking at The Lake District

after Wallace Stevens

Cloud
    fell
        dale
            lake
a pilgrimage of water.

Leave Windermere's Riviera-boated marina
and climb to Dock Tarn – know silence.

The fear of the Lakes is the beginning of wisdom.
Do not take winds, waters, mists, snows, wild weathers
lightly.

Fells are rough waves
cragged with snow.

A raven, higher than Cat Bells,
croaks mockery at my landlocked boots.

Gravity pulls water down,
yet the higher you climb, the wetter.

Easedale Tarn looks up at skies,
plays chameleon, now azure, now black.

'Hiker, why leave the level way
for the rough ride of the fells?'
If you ask that, you're a flat man.

Fjell, dal: once Norsemen strode here.

Herdwicks: brown bodies on strong legs
stand their ground, look you straight in the eye.
Sheep like small brown bears.

Leave your pavement shoes in the flat-foot city.
Let your boots be goat hooves rock-hopping the fells.

Here celebrate all weathers but, when sun shines,
drink blue sky.

Wordsworth's daffodils – a cliche now?
Not here at your feet, not this tiny Spring gold.

Short Summer, Norway

High
wild mountains.
A lake
slap, lap, laps
at my feet,
its far side still snow
and ice floe.
Trees
are inches high,
clinging to cold ground
from colder wind.
A small bird
teeters on a rock's tip
then wheels away
in the wind's whip.
I leave a footprint
in black mud between rocks;
soon snow will cover it,
long nights
enfold it.

Loch Achall

It is the quietness of the sounds:
a sheep's bleat a loch and hillside away,
a fly's wings' rustle near my ear,
the small splash of a smaller fish.
Ripples of water, of air
grow perfect circles
from precise centres.

It is the vastness of the hills,
ben beyond ben to clouds' horizons.
Undulations of bracken and stone
are waves on the flanks of seas.
Mountains and glens make rugged rhythms
of rock mass and air.

A breeze puckers the loch's surface showing
the stillness that is motion,
and the motion that is stillness.

Breaking

Sea rolls

curls

climbs

crescendoes

CRASHES

to cascade

the billion pebbled shore

foam

the drag

the draw

the pebbles roar

Blind Homer

Blind Homer,
was he always sightless?
Had he *seen* the wine dark sea
who saw men's hearts,
their pulsings, currents,
treacherous tides,
who set in aspic
the glitter of men's words,
the murderous surge beneath?

This blind Greek
who viewed Olympus,
sky palace of the macho gods,
saw goddess Pallas Athena
moved for Odysseus
for his wife Penelope,
for their son Telemachus.
She would pilot him
through rocks of Poseidon's wrath
to home again and family
while Odysseus would put to sword
the mocking suitors,
parasites for the pickings.

In the troughs
between the crests of words
did the sightless one see
Pallas Athena as hero,
and hers the wine-dark Odyssey?

Know Why

Moon
round
full
dead rock
alive with light
white
bright
spinnaker billowing
the black sky

Why should
it still matter
for this post-truth
post-nature
digital chatter
clatter world?
Why look up?

Just look up

Know why!

Response

to reading poems by Margaret Atwood

And how shall I write?
How reply? She confides,
her words a call to conversation.
I stall, am dumb.
Why no response to such gold greeting?

She draws aside the curtain of herself,
opens doors I did not know I had.

Her words are spare, sere,
wry as dry beech leaves
yet smell of loam and roots' mycelia.
No sentimentality, no forcing too close,
no hot breath in your face,
no words wasted.

In courtesy, in creativity, in courage
may this ink essay an answer.

It Came

It came silently, looking past me,
but I sensed its aim. It took my arm.
I resisted, but feebly. My blood
seeped into its body, my mind into its face
which did not change. And then the trek
through scrub, through rubble of the lost towns,
crushed fragments of the roaring wars.
I felt the destination, far off. I paused for a piss;
it waited, but its eyes looked beyond horizons.
We walked on, my step faltering, but it showed
no impatience.
                              In the late afternoon
we reached the cliff. The fall was not sudden,
but a slow sinking into greyness, endless.
I remembered, like an old film on damaged reel,
a world it too falling, fragment of a dead meteor,
no navigation, no end, a longer, longer way
from home, that small planet, that smaller life,
those once loves.

Many of my poems, I suppose, tend to be upbeat. This
one came out of a low time. Poetry can express anything
and everything.

Listen

Listen

The Sun is sinking
hear the World roll into darkness

A million light years beyond
uproar of stars
and silence absolute

Like Evelyn Glennie
welcome vibrations

 orchestras

Hear your voice
my voice
our intellects colliding
rebounding

dancing from new angles
to strike again
to delight

Beneath are
profound tremors
our wordless sea-deep language

Listen

It's Quiet When

It's quiet when you go deaf –
a slight singing in your ears, otherwise
it's solitary snow time.
Are all cars electric?
Have birds swallowed their song?
Here is the Silent Spring. Mouths
open and shut – you stare for lip clues.
People smile and look for reply; you nod,
smile back. They think, *Stupid man*.
Full blast, the radio's quiet words are blurred,
fuzzed at the consonants' edges.
Bees are buzzless. Bells go *dong*
as though not to wake you.
Is this peace? Nirvana? Never!
Give me back not just the motorbike's roar,
the ruckus of Saturday night in the city
but the subtle sounds like the lift in your voice
when you say, 'Why not? Yes.'

Fortunately my temporary deafness was cured, but I had been
to that place where many have to live.

Squirrel

Poet Philip Gross's squirrel makes like a squirrel.
Its squirrelness delights him, its quick go-stop-go,
its gymnastics on a tree, its claw-clutch into bark,
its dart between words, its stealing a poem
like a nut to crack.

                    My squirrel unreeled
my knot of knowledge: it swam!
It dog-paddled far from land or tree, heading –
where? My Norfolk Broad was its North Sea.
Will fish climb trees, hippopatami fly?
Was it an utter nutter? I paddled alongside it,
offered it the flat of my blade ... it ran up the shaft,
jumped into my craft, and explored it
unfazed by a man in a hollow log. Then, cold,
it curled itself in the prow of my canoe.

Later, I landed. Squirrel leapt ashore,
ran for the nearest tree, and up. Became again
proper squirrel. Was it relieved? Was I relieved?
Yes, the world had righted itself, magnetic North
no longer South, our feet on dry Norfolk.
Yet I miss that world where squirrels go maritime.
So I will search for fish that clamber conifers,
and duck when I hear the whoomph whoomph whoomph
of the legbeat of flying hippopotomi

Kingfisher
a silly verse

Kingfisher,
blue streaker and a flasher,

does not give a flying f**k
for flotillas of mere mallard d**k,

while white swans imperial
consider it funereal

that cormorants are black as sable.
Fish laugh at such a birdy Babel -

as you may too, if you are able.

Blackbird

Blackbird –
cocky bugga
happy to lug a
poor stretchy, stretchy, getting thinner
ouch! worm out of the ground for dinner.
Any sight of danger, sign of harm
he chink chink chinks his cat alarm.
Beak gold, feathers black;
his mate is brown, the Jill of Jack.
(I question whether Wallace Stevens'
Blackbird – 13 ways, odd not evens –
was something other: raven, rook or chough?
Poetic licence or poetic fluff?)

But my true blackbird's out there on the lawn;
he is my very dusk and dawn.

Goldcrest

Dead goldcrest,
our smallest native bird,
weightless in my hand.
Yesterday, its quick wings and heart
beat fast as a trilled 'r'.

My thumb ruffles breast down,
– warm and subtle colours;
but its crest is gorse-fire
its beak gorse thorn.

I take it home, offer it
as I would a wild flower.
Coddled in my palm,
it is stroked, admired,
felt for.

What to do with it?
We do not wish to see,
or smell, its inevitable rot.
I take it to the back door,
and in a mockery of flight,
lob it into the bushes.

Tonight, smaller creatures,
the nano-jackals of our garden,
will scavenge. Life teems from death,
sharp as gorse thorns,
brilliant as gorse flames.

Herring Gull

Who loves a herring gull?
Who feels empathy towards that
sea-polished-pebble eye?
Gull feels none for me as, swooping,
it snatch-rips out of my shocked hand
my hot and golden potato chip.
It perches on a deckchair back,
insolent, too close. I shout,
wave featherless arms in futile anger.

It observes, shrugs, takes off
with wide-winged ease into air designed
for it, not for ground-bound me.
Yet I admire such nonchalance,
its tight-boned brain not cumbered
by intellect or ethics. Gull ethics? A joke!
But maybe I give it better at being herring gull
than I am at being me.

High in the Ash Tree

High in the ash tree
a jazz clarinetist improvises;
each riff, each phrase
delights the musician
so he plays it quick
again, again. Or is this treble
to delight the young couple
standing close, still,
staring up into the boughs
through the young leaves?

No, but it feels like that
and a long way from the dull dread
of coronavirus
this clear dusk evening.
It's just a bird singing
the way they do,
the way evolution
says it must.
Yet still we thank this unseen
song thrush.

Last Light

Last Autumn light

slides over broad boulder

of horizon.

A tree's

last leaves

sieve light

fretwork of dark and bright.

Take it now,

full sight

before the night,

before the night.

Over

The holiday is over,
key in the door and
back to the old stuff –
mundane.
Doormat littered with junk mail,
the house cold.
You switch on the heating
(it will take time)
find tinned food
(you'll supermarket tomorrow)
unpack and throw grubby clothes
in the washing machine.
You watch it churn and remember,
a thousand miles gone,
that other land.

Old Woman, Alone

Old woman, alone.

She might drag herself from her armchair -
much to do.
Phone a friend, octogenarian,
but she is deaf.
Load herself into her electric chair to visit and shop,
but it is raining.
Clean the kitchen,
but for whom should she cook?
Sort books and clothes for the charity shop,
but who will carry them?

Sitting in her chair she looks at her watch -
another hour dead and buried.

What's Left

Sky blew itself dry and turned blue;
late, but chance for a sunset walk.
As she too was doing.
Elderly, widow now.
I said, 'Hello.'
A few words further and her face crumpled.
She said, 'I try to keep going.'
I said, 'And you do.' She wept
for her dead man and her loneliness.
I walked her home.
At her gate she turned her face
from the setting sun and said,
'Look at the light on those trees.'

Play That Tune

Dementia, and the blank look
of nil recognition...
But play him that number that rocked the late Fifties,
crude, but they jived to it, spun the girls
in their tight-belted shirtwaisters, heels and hairdos.
He was there with the best of them,
sweating under the strobes,
a few beers down and reckoning his chances,
his BSA 500 outside. She on the pillion
he rode her home – via the wood...
Gone midnight, and her dad waiting at the front gate,
ready to give him and the girl whatfor.
Can he remember?
Play that number, watch his face.
Yes, through the brain fog
he's up and alive and dancing
and there again.

An Urgent Honking

An urgent honking. I look up:
two Canada geese wing overhead,
swift in close formation, precision.
They swing left, climb, swoop right,
circle wide, complete an airy lap,
honk sweeping over – no speed check.
Again and again, each circuit a variation,
yet tight formation, wing beats synchronised.
This Red Arrow display thrills,
yet is not for us – this is their challenge
'Can you keep pace and position with me?'
It is their mating dance.

Once, on a sweaty dance floor,
didn't you rock together as challenge, display?
Weren't you wild geese?

Risks

Step out of your front door –
  It's a risk.
Breathe air –
  It's a covid risk.
Change your job –
  Could be risky.
Stay in your job –
  Firm goes bust? Risky.
Marry –
  Now that is a risk.
Have children –
  That's risk multiplied.
Make new friends –
  People are a risk.
Spend your money –
  Future risk.
Invest your money –
  Absolute risk.
Be on this planet –
  Natural risk.
Just live –
  Ultimate risk.

Yes, I'll take the risk.

Versus

Chekhov did not rate
     Sarah Bernhardt;
doubtless she did not rate
     Anton Chekhov –
problem of the intellectual
     playwright against
the act-you-off-the-stage
     celebrity.
Chekhov wrote of disillusion, hypocrisy,
     the repressed spirit;
Bernhardt repressed nothing,
     she let it all out with fireworks.
Chekhov and Bernhardt are long dead,
     regrettably.
If alive, which would I be drawn to?
     Obviously both.

A Giant

A giant among mortals,
Gladstone, William Ewart,
intellectual, liberal High Church,
your energy, your devotion to the Good,
your impeccable morals, yet
grasping a theology which encompassed
a world of cultures, religions, sciences.
Powerful Prime Minister, you were
to your Queen the Most Brilliant of Men
(though your rival, Disraeli, made her feel
the Most Brilliant of Women).

Gladstone, William Ewart
perhaps you lacked humour and charm
but, as I climb the stairs above your great Library
donated for the good of us lesser mortals,
I stop at your bust, life-size, life-like
and cannot help but stroke your nose.

Epitaph for a Tyrant

Shelley, you wrote your 'Ozymandias'
And you may think me just a silly ass
To dare compare your cruel tyrant true
With late – and unlamented – Auntie Pru,
But she struck terror into children's hearts
With oven-baked, tooth-breaking scones and tarts
While we'd to smile and kiss her warty cheek
Then sit so still an hour seemed like a week.
She'd interrogate what we had learned at school
(tricky since we'd mostly played the fool)
And sing with her most dreadful moral hymns
And be told tales more terrible than Grimm's.

She's gone, and now *I'm* Uncle Old Sclerotic.
Hoorah! It's now my turn to be despotic!

Bar in Donegal

A man stands up and sings,
solo, unaccompanied,
his voice peat, lough, heather,
the glisten of the waterfall's long spill,
clouds and their shadows, sunlight
sweeping the valley, the hills.
He sings a history of valour and pain,
faith and betrayal, jealousy and love.

Meanwhile the drinkers talk,
and their talk is free among family,
friends, lovers – yet still listening,
drinking down the songs together
with the white heads
and black bodies
of their Guinness.

Here is Ireland on a Saturday night -
and no hard feelings.

Party

Yes, we'll have a party!
Oh, the power and pleasure of selecting our guests
(and rejecting others). We hope they'll be delighted
and RSVP us *tout de suite,* bringing wine and their five wits...
And here they come some have travelled far.
No problem for Homer (the Greek one) – he's well shipped,
and Geoffrey Chaucer trotting upon a rouncy as he kouthe.
There's Will Shakespeare waving a sheaf of parchment –
it's his brand new comedy titled ... ah, now sadly lost.
And lurching up the street two-eared, a not too drunk
Van Gogh. Here comes striding a young Angela Davies
with full Afro. Is that Jane Austen we spy, arm-in-arm
with a reluctant Emily Dickinson? Listen...a sparrow
with a voice to vibrate Paris: welcome Edith Piaf,
And look, raga-ing up the road, comes a smile with
Ravi Shankar round it. Now I spy God's sweet comedian,
Archbishop Desmond – Tutu to you.
And next – Oh yes! – a selection of girlfriends (ex),
each young as I remember them. Not sure about
bringing their other boyfriends but, well, fair is fair.
Oh, we'll have fun, all of us! Fascinating to see
their surprise and their greetings each to each,
their words growing to a fireworks fiesta.
And soon the music vibrates and the drinks go down,
and there's Homer dancing with Emily Dickinson,
and – yes, you're all invited too!

First Snow

First snow: flakes fall through lamplight,
lit, singular, legion,
soft night invaders, a white joke
for tomorrow's commuters

– who rise
astonished at their cars' restyling,
smooth mantling. They must brush down
to glass and metal with cold-shocked hands.

Tyres spin and slip, cars lurch and crab,
slide back down slopes, crunch into kerbs,
crunch into each other,
block highways, are abandoned.

The ones with snow tyres grip,
treads bite down, hold, direction forward,
laying crisp patterned tracks
Narrowing to road's horizon.

Winter is here.
I pull on boots with deep treads.
I walk, I print.
Read my tracks.

The Linear Poet Longs For

a sane eye *and a mad brain*

a tsunami of images
                                        to surge and spill
                a rainbow to splinter
and shatter

        a cacophony of
                        births
                                deaths
                                        detritus

a beachcombing
                of gaudy plastics
        with evolutions of seashells

                                out of such *anarchy*
                let him write
no logic
                no narrative

                                                but freely associate

                let his smithereens
        make tumbling streams

his disintegrations
                impossible designs

His Anger

His anger burst
   mine explosion
the crash, crush
   and rush of fire

It engulfed family
   scorched
left scars
   on tender skins

His wife *apologised*
   'Must have upset him
something I said
   mustn't nag'

The daughter survived
   years on told her partner
'Do what my Dad did
   and you're gone'

Last Laugh

May trees have the last laugh
although we trash them,
bulldoze the Amazon Forests,
scythe through for HS2,
blast them with man-boosted storms.

Many still stand over us,
pines taller than our dreams,
oaks wider than our vision.
Plunging roots give grip and grasp –
they network through mycelia.

Meanwhile we slip and slither
in superficiality and shake the Earth
with our universal pratfalls.

If ethics count for anything
give back to trees their natural
their living right.

Hear

Question me...criticise me...doubt me,
But hear my words.
Consider them...feel them.

Know the love that drives them.

My roots are coarse...muddy,
But my branches offer you
Leaves...flowers...seed.

About the author

Mike Gower was born in Walthamstow.
After school he trained as a radiographer in
the Royal Army Medical Corps for two years
and, on discharge, worked as a labourer on
building sites.

He applied to read English at the University
of Bristol and to his astonishment was
accepted. He later taught English, drama and
cricket in Bristol schools and in rural
Gloucestershire.

Now he writes poetry, concentrates on open
mic nights, hillwalking, growing things and
his grandchildren.

He believes that poetry can express anything
and everything. This is his first collection.

BV - #0144 - 041124 - C0 - 203/127/6 - PB - 9781739605094 - Matt Lamination